Such Places as Memory

Writing **Architecture**

A project of the Anyone Corporation

The MIT Press Cambridge, Massachusetts London, England

Such Places as Memory

Poems 1953–1996

John Hejduk

The "Sentences on the House" were first read by John Hejduk at the Cooper Hewitt Museum, New York, in the spring of 1993 and were dedicated to John Jay Iselin, President of The Cooper Union for the Advancement of Science and Art.

This book was printed and bound in the United States of America.

Library of Congress Cataloging-in-Publication Data

Hejduk, John, 1929–

   Such places as memory : poems 1953–1996 / John Hejduk.

      p. cm. — (Writing architecture)

   ISBN-10: 0-262-58158-2 (pbk)
   ISBN-13: 978-0-262-58158-5 (pbk)

   I. Title. II. Series.

PS3558.E472S8 1998

811'.54—dc21   97–48920

                                                        CIP

10 9 8 7 6 5 4

Dedicated to Gloria Fiorentino

John Hejduk: Poetry as Architecture, Architecture as Poetry
David Shapiro

John Hejduk is a builder of worlds, in his architectural structures, drawings, and masques, in his inflection and true creation of an experimental school of architectural education at Cooper Union for nearly three decades, and in his astonishingly imbricated texts, which are the none-too-secret keys to his building. If one challenges the normal architectural historian about the lack of subtle critique to date of this giant's work, one usually finds that the critic is lacking in the vital synaesthetic sense that would respond to these fused exercises in spirit. The students of architecture, however, have responded, and a whole generation has been enthralled by the possibilities of a tragic, personal, fragile, truth-telling architecture which is utterly entwined with a poetics at once severe and musical. The uncanny lure of Hejduk's voice, its demotic authority, is something both inimitable and infectious. No one who has ever heard the Dean read his poems or prose or simply speak in his office about the education of the architect—his favorite theme and life-time devotion—can forget the powerful and endearing revelatory accents of that voice. Here, a native-born architecture speaks, be it about seashells, disease, or Delacroix, and Hejduk's indelible writings have built up a cinematic vertigo of these voices, all his own.

His accomplishments as an architect and delicate draftsman are replete, and perhaps the inexhaustibility of his double-guarded works—structures in Oslo, London, Berlin, and Prague, the masques and new chapels—all proceeds from a quite rational critique of the soulless escapades of the whimsical eclecticism that has surrounded and dominated our era, on the one hand, and a wrecked formalism, on the other. Answering Julia Kristeva's plea for an eruptive voice in such a deadened time, Hejduk has gone beyond the mathematical reductions of his permutationally obsessed peers. He is the architect, moreover, who has best reimagined Mies's fabulous geometrical project, and he it is who has most passionately embraced and celebrated the true pathos of Le Corbusier without deliquescence into an insipid expressionism.

To understand the following poems, the student is advised to go to Hejduk's drawings and structures, and to examine vigilantly Hejduk's dazzlingly radical homage to Mondrian, the by now incalculably significant if unbuilt Wall House series, in which a new space is carved from the severest appraisals of neo-plasticism and post-cubist alignments. In these elegiac houses, Hejduk discovered himself as a wild original of the American anti-sublime. He continued in his tremendous and anti-sentimental texts on the Holocaust to reconvene the forces of a poetics within an architecture largely lost elsewhere to gestures of parodistic abandon. Hejduk once told me he couldn't tolerate the word "parody," and his uniqueness lies in being able to create, in a time of parodistic reduction, a complex and ironic style in which parody is elided but a tragic humor still spreads and stains and sustains a mature palimpsest of work. None of the enclosed poems, therefore, is a parody or "New York School" collage; perhaps all are homages— to Michelangelo, to the great myths, and to space itself.

Hejduk is capable of so many different kinds of texts that I simply underline the vital variety of linguistic experience he offers. On the one hand, he is capable of short naturalistic observation reminiscent of William Carlos Williams. Here he reminds us, in fractured cubo-futurist notes, of his continued affection for his roots in the Bronx and of his love for urban realities, which he never forgets, down to the loved detail of an old bus ticket. His best poems start with this precision but are then swept along by a more intransigent tone and structuring drive. His most fateful work, influenced by Rilke and Celan, is unforced but impelled by an energy that emerges from a species of Blakean war. The texts are descriptive, but intimate and angry with stupidity. He is often impelled to speech and drawing by a sense of the "wild emptiness" of contemporary culture, in Arthur A. Cohen's theological phrase. Hejduk's poems then transform into critical allegory, readings within readings, double-guarded dreams of ruined myth. He again reverts to a poetry that is already late or melancholy commentary on Biblical topoi.

I think this work on themes of Adam and Paradise and fallen language is meant to serve as constant deposition against Pop Art and consumerist images of mild hedonism. His best work has the diagrammatic poetry, as Michal Govrin put it in lectures at Cooper Union, of Jewish law. Each one of his compacted works of architecture, as I have often heard him introduce them in his house or school office, is entangled with the strangeness of a story. And this constant storytelling, this strategy of a narrative architect has made his work the densest and most lyrical of any of his contemporaries. He does not build without "characters." Surely, we know architects who have imitated his sculptural Baroque or his endlessly studied geometrical cadenzas. He has been widely imitated and yet, without this vital term of his uncanny acoustic element or his even more hidden cinematic-narrative structuring, the results look oddly depleted in other hands. No architect in our time has created a set of structures, for example his Berlin Masque, that have such a face. As Ingmar Bergman simply darkens the radiance of Liv Ullman in a long take in *Persona*, a silent prolongation of opacity and time, so Hejduk in his terrifying sequences on Riga and Vladivostok makes a protracted series of sculptural-linguistic witnesses to the American darkness.

His last masterpieces are his most simple, yet still oracular, in the sense in which Gershom Scholem said Walter Benjamin spoke always with a grammar of revelation. His late "Sentences on the House" I underline as one of his most refined achievements. I consider these sentences to constitute one of the most superb prose poems, and in a prose rigorous as the early Blanchot. Hejduk in these radiantly halakhic sentences recreates an erotics of architecture, an animation that reinvigorates our sense of the paradoxes of still life. A lifetime of reading and building have culminated here in a fountain of explosive metaphor. But he does not stop with metaphor in romantic excess: metaphor as cosmetic. These last prose sequences of personified houses constitute a liminal ritual that any anthropologist would wish to prolong. They remind us of the most archaic practices, of bodies buried under sites, of the terror of any space, of the antithetical meanings of primary space, to change Freud's uncanny title. Hejduk here creates, as elsewhere in his "Collapse of Time" clock of deletion, a ceremony to the act of and art of architecture, that fragile art. His books will outlast many cities.

*

When I first met John Hejduk decades ago at the Institute for Architecture and Urban Studies, I already knew his immaculately piercing experiments, but I did not know his poetry. We met with a skeptical exchange that he would show me his poems and I would show him "my architecture." My skepticism was replaced by admiration, particularly for his utter commitment to the space of language. At the Cooper Union, for example—the best working space in New York City, as Francesco Pellizzi has observed—he was the first architectural pedagogue to insist that all his graduates, trained in the most rigorous structures course that exists, meet and train with poets, anthropologists, and surgeons to rethink architecture as a fundamentally multiple mode. I was persuaded by him to turn to the school for twenty years as a place to "teach" Rimbaud, Baudelaire, Pessoa, Pasternak, and Wallace Stevens, as ways to initiate a study of cities and to inflect new architectural forms. Our students built sestinas, built in the condition of Tu Fu as you would build in the condition of Juan Gris. Along with the almost completely unknown school of Ritoque, Chile—a school I have only recently learned of through the beautiful text *The Road That Is Not a Road*—I can think of no school more dedicated to the fundamentally surrealist principles of convulsive beauty than Hejduk's. He often says how much he despises the fashionable taste for chaos, and he embraces no flattering dogmas, such as the redemptive role of computers. His drawings, his school, and his poetry have initiated an architectural vocabulary without true recompense. A whole historical investigation remains to be done on the influence of this idea of architectural education, the most experimental haven since Black Mountain College. Its graduates and professors have been chosen by Hejduk not to betray architecture into something reductively literary or into critical jargon or dogma. Hejduk despises jargon and loves thought, and it is the tectonic in poetry he celebrates. These colloquial poems attest to his humble Thomas Hardy-like love affair with the life of detail and form. His witty eyes sparkle here in coruscating lines of life.

Poetry and architecture are not just contingent analogues for Hejduk. They are both building arts. They are ontologically the same art, as he has proposed a drawing strong as a building and vice versa. Poetry is not confession, an ejaculatory mode of expressionism. Nor is it dominated, in Roman Jakobson's sense, by the axes of reference or a resort to public, political command. Poetry and architecture are both replete arts of repetition and persistence, and no one knows better than Hejduk the haunting uses of parallelism in all its devious asymmetries, first pointed out in Hebraic poetry by one Bishop Lowth. The sculptural sense of an authoritative text is built up by Hejduk, for example in his late "Sentences on the House," exactly by this commandeering of parallelism. The geometry of his most insistent architectural projects, for example his Diamond Houses, is a fundamental partner of his exacting parallelisms here. This is what Jakobson meant by "the poetry of grammar and the grammar of poetry." Here, Hejduk builds up poems of a geometrical fury. Such a poetry does not depend on the ornament of rhyme or conventional meter, but it does depend on the fundamental cosmology of geometric repetition with drastic differences. Furthermore, such poetry does not need to sacrifice any of the so-called "axes of the aesthetic." One still has here a poetry of truth-telling detail and sensuous palpability. The poetry is maximal and severe, and the poems build up in sequence to the final variable structure: the book. The project of the Mallarmean book, the encyclopedic synoptic Thing, the book of the twentieth century and beyond, is implied in all of Hejduk's masques, drawings, and poems. Architecture and poetry point to the fabulous eternity of the Book, and the drive of Hejduk's sequential drawing-cities and structured imaginary-real worlds are all to underline a tumultuous vision of this Anthology.

This book is, as I like to insist, one of the keys to Hejduk's immense accumulations of works in a relay of media. His fecundity is principled, and these poems stand as rather condensed illuminations of a vaster terrain of building and thinking. The friend of such work is advised to return to the pleasure of those architectural books, such as *Bovisa*, *Mask of Medusa*, *Vladivostok*, *Soundings*, *Adjusting Foundations*, and perhaps, above all, of *Victims*—the titles themselves like little severe poems—and learn with Hejduk how architecture(s) do indeed fall in love. His immensely plural work has an uncanny unity and is never about the delights of the dilettante. Rather, with De Chirico, a painter and novelist, the delights of the poet are meditations of disappearance in "the worst century so far." Who among Americans has been capable of reinstating the structure as tragic monument, and who has most dedicated himself to the darkest proposition: Lost is lost? With his beloved Dickinson, Hawthorne, and Melville, he has made out of that principle of American darkness a consolation and a calling.

Prayer for a House
for J.H.

Blessed is the architect of the removed structures
Blessed is the structure that weathers in spring snow like lies
Blessed is the crystal that leaps out of the matrix like a fool
And blessed is the school

Blessed factures
Blessed like spring snow
Blessed like a fool
And burnt book

Is the school a structure or weather
Or a lie like spring snow
And is the matrix leaping also like a fool
And is the book built or burnt?

Blessed is the removed
Blessed too the inlay like spring
Blessed is the tiger of the matrix like a found fool
And blessed the unbuilt like a book

Blessed is the architect who survives all removal
Blessed is the trapped structure like a gift
Blessed is the crystal fool
And blessed is the school

Blessed is the cut and the cry
Blessed the body of the patient in spring snow like lies
Blessed is the crystal stepping out of the matrix like a fool
And blessed is a burning book

Blessed is the anchorite and the architect in the dark smudge
Blessed is the remover bending to remove
Blessed is the folly leaping out of matrix
And blessed is the empty center

Blessed burning structures
Blessed like snowy spring
Blessed cry blessed in the matrix like a cut fool
And blessed each unlit book

Blessed is the architect of the removed cut
Blessed the structures that weather in lies like spring snow
Blessed is the crystal that leaps out of the matrix like a fool
And blessed is the school, like a burning library

Old new prayer
Old new song
Blessed is the crystal and the cry and the matrix like a painting fool
And blessed is the school

Such Places as Memory

The Hesitation of Orpheus

During the night
as the snow
descended
it turned to
blood
transforming
the river to the
color
of mahogany
the ocean remained
Prussian blue
when the starfish
floated upward
As soulfilaments
released
from undersea
volcanoes
the moon became
an ellipse
before collapse
the flames of the sun
froze
when Orpheus
began his turn
to his horror
Eurydice
continued her journey
towards him
kissing death

A shudder ran through
the wings of the angel
causing the air to chill

Orpheus's Memory

She pleaded her case
and the fog amplified her cries
Heurtebise taught her how to float
one inch above the ground
he placed his arm around her waist
so she could feel her weight
the departure slipped through his fingers
Eurydice proceeded towards him
intent on his disappearance
he tried to capture the sound
of her deathmemory
she tore apart the strings
of his lyre
her heart burst red roses

Diana

The arrow enlarged
the heart in the back
Diana lowered her bow
The string was cut
A wind moved her cape
covering the face
His hand slipped
from above
Boots tipped a branch
It without sound
became
cold sepia

Annunciation

The Angel dropped
and knelt
to ask a pardon
for its announcement
anticipating the
coming entombment
The stone vault door
exploded into
putrid passage
Italian was softly spoken
The cloth was loomed
in iris
Waxed banisters
pinioned the entry
Impregnation was complete
Joseph wept

Bacchus

the stone sea shell
envelops a granite
window pane
the marble Bacchus
uplifts the solid goblet
arm veins brush the grapes
eyes convolute
circular incisions
made from within
Saint Anne contemplates
fabrics and limbs
disengagement follows
voided contours
vacuums fill the pores
seepage is inevitable

Saint Anne Content

at first there was no lamb
nor its ear pulled
by the immaculate child
only Saint Anne's finger
pointed upward in a one
the small evolving Christ
genuflecting those to be
communioned in a Turner light
Mother Mary's smile
proudly satisfied
Jesus' trunk emerging
from the arms cloth
Anne's face chalk rendered
receives eye sockets
winged shaped voluminous
then the lamb appears
in pain child
enjoying the touch
silk covered legs intertwined
Mother Anne's melancholia sensed
the mist veils
an Italian landscape
clouds smother the echoes
a golden angel goes forward
backwards
wings wrapped as a shroud

Florentine Grey

His thoughts elicit silent response
Bruges Madonna's Carrara lips
polished by tips of fingers
gently allowing stone pores to breathe
His mother has wept
marble before
Lorenzo's elbow rests upon a casket
his hand presses a mouth
while suspending a cloth
Giuliano's neck muscles taut
yet bent towards a niche
Locks flood the ear
Aurora suppresses a sigh
Giorno face owl countenance
Crepuscolo accepts the cuts
Notte slips into the shade
Medici woman offers a breast
Christ's arm is separated
split from
the Rondanini Pietà
He is kept from descending
by a pull of a heart

A Dutch Interior

the mandolin intestines of
hollowed black crystals
slide against the internal
curvature
ultimately released through
the hole of stretched fibers
held
then diminished
in a tap

Duet

whippet dogs growl
when boys bring
hot wine
through teak arches
her finger caresses
an ivory key
parchment is felt
perched parrot sleeps
bracelet wrists
below folded cuffs
bows limp
on nape down hair
his finger pulls
the silk string
three-quarter framed
landscape foretells
a Dutch storm
all eyelids
lowered to a
spinet sound

Without Interior

lie long grand odalisque
turban askew pillow indented
cyclop eye dead center
to face three-quarter view
edge of lip diminish
to a puncture
braided hair follows
contour of ear
circumference spine sweeps
twenty degrees southwest
in shade breast armpit stomach
fur silk flesh converge
to hollow blush
brown of peacock feathers
in cave between
hand palm and leg calf
toes feel painted metal
silver cask spouts dry yellow mists
1814 is painted on cobalt blue
triangles shift as in a sea

To Madame D'Haussonville

there are no reflections
within Madame d'Haussonville
only opacities which sink
into the cloth and folds
of a Fuseli monster
the arm holds the drapes
of a hidden birth
the flower vase
perpetuates the myth
her smile shames Leonardo
red bow the wait
hands are suspended
that never scratch the earth
but tip the tongue
for infusion
dare that breast be held

On a Bridge

lions sit like dogs
sphinx knew the lot
travertine bridges hold
vertical quiescent wings
hung
tuxedo jackets with
four holes
at what point do
the feathers become flesh
it is difficult to paint
the backs of heads
tails drag infiltrated
with dust
in the resurrection rest home
a falcon beak bent
carbolic fish encouraged
the derbied head slit
mouth moistened
the hands fondling
beads of grey lint
within the winter
coat pocket
flaps open
a sulphur light
is washed aqua marine
it is the leaded line
which reflects the graphite

Oslo Room

Limp flesh arm
and black hair
extend towards the floor
Perhaps the wrist bleeds
into the palm
or is it the
red of paint
brushed in
She lies two degrees
down from an exact
horizontal
her white blouse open
sweet breast exposed
The mattress cover
billows
from the fold
A weighted black stocking
concaves turquoise blue
silk blanket
The heavy cloth of skirt
bent under knees
pyramid thrust
The Siena bed
slides deep
Although drunk or dead
mouth nose eyes
might be kissed

The Metronome

sounds in deep perspective
barreling within spirals
forward dart
upon the frame
of time ellipses
the brass metronome
cask of oak
the pendulum stuck
at thirty-two degrees
the ovality of
a silence
a high chair matron
observes the note
the wood shutters meet
the iron grille at
one hundred and eighty
the corner statue
indeterminate definitely small
tends to fold
in upon itself
the triangular sliver
overlooks the singular
ivory key
densities silently implode

France Is Far

etched cows move
towards vertical banks
one slips on the rail
or is it the horizon line
that must be the house of Caleb
les deux pigeons kissed on the terrace
the military man paid the waiter
she looked through the double hung
window east side
the el shades had become warped
the catboat entered the squall
naked men tended the tiller
he read the paper in the park
at 10 p.m.
a wreath nailed to the door
of an isolated brownstone
in an earth lot sumac rendered
two children dug while
awnings were lowered
the carriage approached the mansion
near Vestal he closed the barn doors
they seemed elegant while living
in Washington Square
a nude woman with slippers
sits in the velvet chair
hands crossed under
the evening lights
early Sunday morning brown
cast iron fascias absorb the heat
those shop fronts are in Secaucus
there is a smell of rotting antiquity
the barber poles tell of France is far

pharmacies diners and florists
always turn the corner
Vermeer was looked at
solitude is a place
ground swells are of gelatin
usherettes doze under wall lamps
Cape Cod dogs bark in the evening
frosted glass doors remain closed
at first she could be from Rouen
yet some Canadians look American
1930 underwoods are heavy
although Léger could have painted her
the granite quarries of Deer Isle
had long since been abandoned
the stonecutters blue prints
were still brittle
don't talk to me of Blackwell's island
you can find that apartment block
only on the edge of Bolzano
the shingle covered turreted house
has gone to sea
the sail comes from Le Havre
the woods are pine dark

Nature Morte

He thought he heard
it enter the still life
although the shutters
were closed
He sat in the wood chair
and waited
for the return
He dreamed of the
cliffs of Le Havre
The rooms somehow
were always permeated
in greens and browns
Suddenly
a lone gull
silently flying appeared
wings interweaving
within the vertical stripes
of the wall paper
His soul was released
inside
it became white

Outside Rome

it stopped when
sheep shadows
mixed with those
of cypresses
the thirty-nine arches
shaded the statues
at sixty degrees
horse pedestals
held bronze hoofs
Ardeatine whispers
skimmed the earth
the photos bled

Venice (1953)

long wait
from blackness
to the blue
anticipation
of dawn
morning breeze
through
dark windows
chalk white
waters
frozen moss
voices
bird and man

Lampasas Square

stillness of heat
blue that does not move
clouds that do not echo
darkness that holds
endless twirl of fan

Cefalù After Lago Negro—Waco Time

The porcelain footprints
moistened in the room
The comforter slid over
the skins
Dark breasts fall
from erect hands
Hail pricked the Porsche
English ladies sipped
chocolate
A cyclist raised
his helmet
Paestum overlooked the sea
A gull flew softly
within the sphere
its wing tip gently
incising the internal membrane
revealing an impression
on the external convexity
Lire were lined up
and counted
on the unsheeted mattress
Mr. White on white inquired
of the other's wife
He refused to acknowledge
the snake
Cactus milk heals the wound
The odor necessitates opening
train windows double hung
A Chinese pagoda outside
of Palermo needed painting
Baedeker insisted upon visiting
the church interior
was filled with cooking utensils

its earth floor kicked
up by hoofs
The altar winter covered
with black cloth
like an armchair
Termini baths seemed salted
water lapped the wood
Cefalù cathedral eroded
against the cliff
corridors emptied by a whisper
The virgin might have come
from Lago Negro
Rather than prolong the stay
take a night ferry
Waco Time

La Roche (1972)

October
La Roche
in the evening
a ritual of darkness
garden stone sunken
a hall chilled
pulpit empty
a choir of silence
black marble opaque
a fireplace vague
hearse lamp lit
the whiteness
of the still
the mortuary slab
the falcon in the niche
color of walls
transforming
from peach to pink
from mauve to brown
leather gloves being buttoned
in the park
a motorcycle gliding
upon crumbled gravel
the Bugatti polished
upon the rack
paintings rotting
in a garage
the smell of ash roses
red chalk powder
in a line on a sill
children sliding
down

a ramp curved
a tuxedo moving
through
metal doors
slamming
echoes in perspective
diminishing to a revelation
it is best not to speak of it
dawn is
Square Doctor White

Helsinki Warehouses

the charcoal cathedral
absorbed the reflections
the trolley cars carried
no passengers
the carrots shriveled
in wooden caskets
the small fish were
packed in blood
sealed in
plastic containers
the fishmongers wore
black leather jackets
and rocked in their barks
the taxi drivers wore
double-breasted coats
with military buttons
one and a half hours
to Moscow
lake punks crystallize
near the park path
there are empty shops
containing old sewing machines
the owner of
the Merano theater
turned the key left
at the end of the tale
the candle extinguished
book pages hung
from the rope
with clothespins
land is to be rented

exterior amphitheaters
look on to
white drainage ditches
coffee trucks sat
in the square
fortifications hardened
the silence
slip out while you can

Oslo Hotel

the cod lies
black hat in hand
birds walk
the palace swoops
the theater
flames in cups
before the doors
a road divides
the metal hospital
from the stone cemetery
wood huts
decay in moisture
removed from hills
fogs filter the cries
near the lake
the Bishop set sail
for Rome
the bark four
inches above the tide
and returned

Berlin Looms

the vanished can
still be felt
banal stanchions
of rusting concrete
envelop the outline
stretched wire produce
the void
air can be blue
the smoke geometric
ice cream licked
from the rafters
the obelisk was moved
on axis
the dry bark of
linden trees split
across the street
the moist shadow
of barges rippled
october ash felled
the pharmacist's cough
drops bought
for a mark
the black eagles swept
the boulevard clean
the canal became
a gelatin
the plan had been
erased

A Miniature Volume

how much does
your heart weigh
I don't know
perhaps as much as
a miniature volume
I would have to turn
it inside out
like a leather glove
my grandfather gave
me a sea conch
to hold I dropped it
stuck like a top
under the drift log
an armadillo shed tears
he held the fishing knife
and split the violin
down the middle
put his hand inside
and removed the air
the limp gut strings
entangled jelly fish
nets slipped and
smothered the swells
a dead sailor
filled with water
like a glass vessel
a widow walked
exhaling iris aromas
she reached out
and hugged the fog
to her breasts
light beam caressed
moist surfaces
night lips blow
sound Nantucket horns

Arcadia

europa rides
a bronze bull
her metal hand
touching his
erect tongue
lily pods push
up against the
spring ice membrane
convex thighs of
cast girls spread
for an inscription
weathered copper green
small breasts emerging
a statue dances
flute to lips
in a marble shell
off axis the court
egyptian granite lion
waits to be removed
spigot mouth fish
rise with the whale
two arms extended
with stretched skin pit
she wraps her iron stained
locks around
winter polished fingers
it must be clay
which molds that
slight stomach bulge
all youth float
upwards from the pool
encased in frozen
stalactites of water
he walks at 6 a.m.
towards the serpentine
the sculptor knew
the northern architect

P.S. 47. BX. 1936

I confess
I was born
in the Bronx County
That it had worn trolley cars
painted yellow, green, and red
That the Bronx
had six-story apartment houses
which were singularly isolated
in empty lots
surrounded by weeds and poison ivy
That there were window awnings
upon the silent cubes
That the trolley cars ran
from Westchester Square
to West Farms
That there was
a Catholic protectory
where the boys wore
long-sleeved shirts
with open collars
and large black high shoes
brown knee socks
which fell down
upon open shoelaces
some wore knickers
That the men of the Bronx
wore caps
and rolled paper rectangles
for their tobacco
That there was a Dr. Black
who stitched poorly
and a Dr. Lynch who pulled
swiftly

That the trolley sped
through streets where all
the actors
of a movie house
were dark
That vegetable wagons and laundry carts
were pulled
by slow horses and four wheels
and the I cash clothes man
shouted
"I cash clothes"
That the Bungalow Bar man
was new
lucky sticks were to be had
in his cold compartment
That concrete stoops were sat upon
and penny candies
could be had
for a penny
That there were people
named Uncle and Aunt
That coffins were in the living room
That pinochle was in the dining room
wind was passed and matches were lit
hearses were black
cemeteries were green
the radio brown
the phono white
That Japanese beetles existed
were plucked from roses
and dropped
into the kerosene jar

That British lead soldiers existed
and could be had
for one dollar fifty a box
of eight
four if they came upon horses
School was for Mr. Shapiro
who taught in the day
and sold Sunday suits at night
When rafts sank
boys drowned
among punk reeds
of dead creeks

CU 1947

Swedish torment and Horn and Hardart
Entwistle sipped from the vested straw
Felt Fedoras and winter coats
Pencil stubs accounting credits
Her teeth fell from her mouth
upon the couch
Beauregards frame and Bible House
Irving Place and Newman Club
The Priest's confessional breath blew
swinging tits and bobby socks
Dylan Thomas and Alex Nevsky
Mott Haven leads straight for
Saint Mary's Park
Old man Fetig wraps the carp
Pluck the chicken salt the pail
Tub butter hardens in oak vats
It's the Greeks who have the concession
on Sassetta Franks
Darby Dent swept the court
The smock of Delaney revealed
the pigeon's neck
was swiftly cracked and dropped into
a shoe-shine box
Pointy shoes and blunted brush
Black trench coat and blue ear muff
Temperas black and white
That one in the pin stripe suit
is a mother-fucker
I always thought so
Not that one the other

Slushed snow under rotting Els
The Ginny Lind fish are to be
moved to Brooklyn
The book-sellers dispossessed
Cincinnati Dancing Pig
Bowery drones Mac trucks
Cheese blintzes finish your soup
The Church of All Nations
Third Rome

Texas (1954)

He designed a church
where his own coffin
couldn't fit through the door
Water color prevailed
I have known you for five years
and I still think
you are a chicken shit
My Thesis is a crematorium
and my Father is an undertaker
The master of Lockhart
is ninety-six today
The Blue Norther froze
the sand upon the sills
The Lampasas jail
waited for the bus
The corrugated metal baked
as the shadow grew
Guadalupe Boogie Woogie
was painted under a fluorescent
The Great Dane upstairs
pushes the marble over the floor
with his snout
I am a member of the FBI
and I live upstairs
you live downstairs
He crushed the beer can
with the stump of his arm
Mountain lions are within
the City Limits
and tarantulas are
on the screen
When the locusts flew
into town
they slept upon the asphalt
pick-up trucks popped them

Bull dogs wept when
crickets fell
Armadillos sniffled when
gloves released
the four-year-olds
cried
The beetles went for the eyes
It's a radar zone
you got to keep your mind
on the speedometer
Shake your sheets
the scorpions are no good
if you're allergic
He counted the tongue and groove
wood ceiling slats
and found it odd
Nigger head clam labels
were changed too
in 1954
Give a little clap to Jesus
Paul Cret designed this building
My God! you're sitting in his chair
and he likes Tigers Milk
It's not exactly Todi or Leonardo
but it will have to do
She really loves me
but that damn Town Planner
is in the way
The rocking chairs of Waco
are half way in between
When you come enter her
in Texarkana
I am taking a freighter
out of Galveston
should be in Yugoslavia
in about five weeks

Out From Lampasas to Odessa

The rocking chair is the soul
of the porch
remove it and all you have left
is white pine for the carpenter ants

Cornelliana (1960)

When in Florence
the President's wife dreamed
of Ithaca
he of Russia
Some drowned men
were never recovered
from the chasm
of iced water and glacial rock
The merry-go-round
near the lake moved
in the summer without inhabitants
The Engineer's behind
bulged over the toy train
called the Allegheny Express
There are spots in Rock Creek
as shallow as a belly button
The snow begins in October
and lasts through April
It is as white as Melville
and as deep as Ahab's pain
The grey houses are those
that are not for sale
The Mass is practiced somewhere
in the trailer camp
Some surveyors never measure
the return
The frozen wood bridges
harden the shells of termites
He is a bird expert
I wish the cat didn't have
to cross his property

The rat approached the barrel
and was blown against the wall
The gas pump is by the pine grove
The music school is up Caleb's fork
The wax is encased in the barn
You have to bury them below
five feet deep
otherwise they might get
I will be gone a few days
lock the cellar door
The Heller House
encloses the portrait of Dryden
Deep greens within polished browns
drizzled mists pervade the rooms
Fogs release the damps
White girls in white frocks
play upon the organ
Wardrobes remain shut
as the blinds
I shaved upon the marble
at 5 a.m.
Proper English Italian
and Argentines enter
The dancing bear
went to New York
The farm houses are not
for farming
The canal carpenters knew
the method
Make it of wood
and paint it white

Northern Tiers

Kiss your own
candle out
The sons of Krakow
pulled their rubbers on
They genuflected to
the Irish Bishop
Creosote timber soiled
the bogs
Steel tracks ossified
Anthracite dust and lake snow
invaded the vaulted hall
Lackawanna benches became
emptied pews
Barge captains dropped
from the falls
two hundred feet
Only acanthus lamps
were lit
The bronze buffalo brooded
Trainmen talked about
the lodge
The freighter funnels
waited in the lock
ice informed the hull
Catholic spires pricked
the lowered cloud
Antiquity was only
two hundred years old
Blacks stared through
muslin shades
Isosceles roof capped
One station of the cross
had been removed

Bus Ride Through

Don't walk red
lit the snow
of an empty school
yard wire fenced
motorcycled left tracks
rippled white
hands black leathered
covered the bars
beam illuminated
granite window arches
moisture silted the
crevice smoke and fog
womb infiltrated
Mount Morris park
brownstone entries
sheet aluminum nailed
tractor man treads
roll a brick
his grey interior shielded
by green eye awnings
copper skinned from
steel bones
Harlem hearses
always parked
middle of the block
its people's cerebellums
covered by
uneradicated ash
all dates implode
the garbage cans
internally scorched by
pine stick fires

it is the absence
of a wall
that penetrates
figures perpetually whispered
to be silent
God damned intravenous
social encyclicals
blue-frocked sisters
of mercy blow
an oval breath
plaster peels
urine analyzed
stopped up kidneys
fill the lungs
Hospital of joint disease
moan a loss

A Monster Slain

out from a painted cardboard cave
two-legged dragon leash held
1918 triplane like wings
rigid to a chicken body
drops blood to clover ground
pierced through the ear
by a wood lance
Uccello's white charger
gallops legs up foreshortened
knight's foot spur suspended
metal elbow discs spin
the breast plate
horse head exposed teeth
clouds form a soft conch
black smoke
rose petal shaped
Saint George no more than fifteen
her cloth Della Francesca blue
there were such things

A Birth

cut stems of flowers fall
Venus is born
full grown woman
she discreetly covers
a convexity pastel tipped
while hair hides hair
bone shell casts the shadow
a Baroque cape is offered
by vine wrapped Madonna
straw ends blow
to a distant landscape
a convolution of
calves and thighs
move in flight
she encircles his waist
their wings fixed in a glide
neck knotted fabrics
moulded into a plaster frieze
in November rust reeds bloom

Silk of Sprigs

no ground flowers are crushed
by gentle Botticelli women
an arrow head of flame
is pulled by the blindfolded
child angel and projected
at finger-entwined graces
they dance the sleepwalkers' circle
apples are glazed with honey
iridescent aquas filter through
ancient umber banks
thorned stems are held in
willing mouth of Siena
the wind rising cut from stone
as wings made of pewter
shards immeshed
in arched trunks
he is a color of scent
pearl bluegrey entombment
she flees in transfixed haste
all swirls lead to a mound
a hand plunges into petals
the flushness of a face
above the oval northern wreath
a benediction is anticipated
Mercury carries a Saracen sword
suspended from the shoulder
his wand announcing
the coming of future fertilities

An Umbrian Passage

tree growth from stone
Joachim's sadness stuns
shepherd's suspicion incite
the leaping dog
lambs sniff hard earth
in front of the hut
his vision is observed
a kiss is given near
the bridge by the gate
black shrouded woman waits
bridal procession enters
an Umbrian passage
a finger slips into a ring
a flute is blown
why does the angel beckon
the way to Egypt
white ribboned wrapped
body of Lazarus
set to an upright
two boys replace the lid
celebrate his coming Jerusalem
a prisoner is taken embraced
by golden Judas
all winged creatures fluttered
on that day of gambled robe
ears hand covered in lamentation
the soldiers slept as he left

Olive Trees in Ochre

difficult to remember face of Mary
Duccio hesitated to paint
the slaughter of the innocents
disciples fled in fear
coals were burnt on long iron shafts
spikes extracted wet oak wood
gold disc tableau heads of grace
lutes plucked songs sung no sound
Blessed Agostino Novello
flew to child resurrections
crucifixion ladder steps one foot apart
Lorenzetti architecture half scale
to full-size protagonists
the jug was filled in
fountain trough while he read
the plasterers built the tower
during the night in dark pink
Bartolo was unable to draw camels
Sassetta monks felt the graces
olive trees died in ochre earth
ship of broken masts
sailors prayed on deck
angels shattered Catherine's wheel
mercenaries paid to keep the peace
three Saints abandoned
Hospital of Mother of the Stairs

Tuscan Wheat

John Hawkwood made of marble
Frescos of Prato receive a virgin
she carries her own halo
while ascending isometric stairs
cut away prosceniums project
Mary's orange hallucinations
Saint Etienne argues disputations
winds blow Noah
crossbows stretched and loaded
San Romano's empty helmets
all move to a hidden vanishing point
hares and dogs leap from the wheat
Niccolò of Tolentine sets
his soft red hat
grey dead horses
in sun's last light
he of Ciarda dismounted
Micheletto's plumed riders prepare
to leave the varnished frame

Saint Ursula's Dream

the pearls of Christ and necklaces of Mary
protrude from lacquered wood
seven dragon heads bellow
from one antelope body
she carries a golden chalice
as blood cascades from her
closed lips Jacobello understood
black tile angels carried the heads
the agony in the garden
winged youths formed the orchestra
Bellini mourners held the Mother
monk processionals paced the square
grape baskets shouldered by blacks
met celebration of the Miracle of the Cross
contradiction of Virgin with Child
blue cape friars flee wounded
lion in peacock walk
Saint Jerome turns to stone while
waiting burial on the floor
wooden drawbridges chain suspended
Saint Ursula had a dream
while Orpheus played the lute
Saint Mark is removed
Andrea born to conceive a Malcontenta
miracle is raised as she adjusts
somnambulists of clowns observed
Punchinello in the nuns' waiting room
Tarantellas danced as Longhi sketched
tricorner hat fixes a point
from white mask pendulum shape
swings above mauve satin
shoes two-inch heel
camp bull's horn pulled by ropes

marking the day of "The Triumph of Asia"
silver chandeliers float from
corkscrew supports cards fall
room smell of wax wall fabrics and musk
faces hidden by ovals ear attached
gentle men bow assignations sealed
how can there be still shadows
paintings lit Guardi tells all

Creation of the Animals Before Braque

Jacobo of Venice nods
his approval his
skullcap loose
Vulcan kneeling lifts
and slides transparencies
along the inner thighs
of promised Venus
her face in afternoon torpor
toes as long as fingers
so spoke he of Finland
black funnel reflected in
circular mirror balanced on
tangent point to spread
Cupid sleeps stomach up
his wings cradled
between flesh and wood
floor disc in perspective
drawn to a hollow vanishing
in a cubic-hedge
Susanna's ablution complete
she touches soft instep
old man twins fold their arms
damp garden sun dry
Saint Mark's body found
then lowered from cantilever
wall suspended sarcophagus
pilasters Sansovino conceived
all equestrians including angels
take cover under vaulted arcades
oak supper table A-framed
built by the son of a carpenter
geese rise from the Brenta
Torcello women scrub the cross
widows walk to wind mills

Palladio Plans

when there was no sun or snow
his buildings were built in autumn
pewter skies molded their outline
the snake road under the flat arc
ended perpendicular to a closed gate
central stairs prevented entry
six columns ionic
entablatures triangular weighted
flower urns found on broken sills
frontal lawns are sometimes cut
porticos and verandas shadow shrouded
marble statues picked by hand
placed on roofs Malcontenta
Thieni is block solid
let there be no illusions
courts filled with still
air of melancholia
fusions of light float granite
empty squares of dust erosion
curtains mark a disappearance
palace barns drained clean
facade brick made from earth souls
braided rope frieze of bone horns
face stone mask reverberate
throughout plaster covered vaults
Veronese lies in fabricated doors
Cloister of Cypresses void of cypress
La Rotonda looks over all death
Teatro Olympico forgive us

Horn Head of Burnt Offerings

He dances promptly
with all no exceptions
bone sticks hit drum
long past old
creations and temptation
Emperor sadly goes
Popes crown Kings
Cardinals receive Bulls
Bishops wished talk
woman fled hour
stretched hooded Abbess
Gentleman lifts a sword
Canon enter a Cathedral
Judge and Advocate alike
bell for the Priest
candle for the Nun
water Physician inspected
look dark Astrologer
Merchant Knight Count
Holbein etch a deluge
build your Babel tower
a mercy seat awaits
the lighting of candelabra
Horn head of burnt offerings
brazen serpent spirals
crucifixions round staff
Ruth gathers the wheat
Amasa embraced by Joab
host Angel struck down
Isaiah already predicted
Bramante Purcell and Morley

Berlin Winter Mask

tops are spun
dropped by boys
in winter's earth
from cord sticks
the procession of
elevated wood chairs
announces an exit
fish skins peeled
revealing a whiteness
all statues gently
linen cloth covered
pregnant women are
accosted they
hold the canes and
empty metal bowls
sepulchre masks
are raised to
count the berries
pillow and bed
support the crucifixion
Carthage lions cry
Medusa's lips close
a thirst for well water
hand plunged in
red waist sack
bagpipes unblown
boar head spitted
as oak barrels roll
five of clubs abandoned
with eggshells and bone
play a tune on
a miniature mandolin
present her with

a turnip necklace
pink carts green wheels
bake the breads
dance the dance
of suspended tents
all windows face
a northern square
sheared at the center
implosions begin
the heavens' evaporation
pewter night stars
nailed through plaster
flood the intervals
with blood
a hymn is hummed

Victims

The unacceptability of the
               erasures
and of the unaccountable
               disappearances
wherever and whenever
               throughout the world.

Victims II

The rains of eternity
can not wash away the blood.

The unspeakable must
fill our lungs
so that
in our exhalation
we blow and breathe
outward
an unearthly lamentation.

At that moment
the word forgiveness
lost its sound
on earth
and in heaven?

Do not make comparisons
our vocabularies
do not have the right.

Lost are lost.

They fell
into the earth
forever.

His heart was so heavy
that
he was unable to carry his soul.

Weigh the silence
enough
to free the sun.

The past is not past.

Atomic Light

Hiroshima
bleaches the very shadows
the evaporation of white
protons, electrons, and neutrons
in disarray as when the
hive has lost its Queen
the bees flying in cacophonic
panic
their terror
of abandonment.

Parallel Implosions

Don't talk to me
of the world as sphere
I know better
It's a frozen cube
of ice melting
We seek the few
air bubbles inside
so we can inhale
the cold throughout
our interiors as to
balance the rigid
encasement of our
extremities
We shout out the
echoes which return
as shards of memory
prying open the sealed
lips releasing
tears that glaze
our internal organs
Talk to me of implosion
which collapses us
inside out
all three dimensionally
condensing to a point
Berlin's Einstein laughing
to an infinity.

Up There

That death in Groningen
made me uneasy
for it was my own
the suddenness of its arrival
made me sit down
the apology was in the knowledge
that it had happened
the others made believe
it had not entered
they continued to talk
although they had taken notice
of my silence
they hastily threw the images
into the box
handed over the umbrella
and hoped for early departure
the scarf was laid
loosely around the neck
a passage was made
down the corridor
there is a taxi waiting
the cabman was English
he talked of the night blue
of the town sky
we both knew the moment
was still to pass
"Do you want me
to accompany you across?"
"There is no need to."
the porter tapped the bell
the elevator had two doors
the porcelain light switch
protruded and clicked

It made no sense
to remove the clothes
sat up straight
on the bed till dawn
fingering the paper
train schedule to Amsterdam
"Sir, a milk with biscuit
jam if you wish"
the phone rang
"Hello? Hello?"
"This is Van Dijk
you had a problem in Groningen?"
"Yes, I died there."

The Sleep of Adam

1
At that precise moment
the illumination
of the body
inside
provides the internal
light
for Death's entry
so that he is able to search out
the soul

The heart was kissed
inside

2
Our Death's wish to play
brass instruments
the flute reminds them
of themselves
by their music they mean
to silence God

On the first note
he sent out the angels
they drew in outline
with the tips of their wings
the sphere of the earth

3
His bones exposed
white grey
he beats the drum
suspended from his
polished spine

the convexity of his
rib cage encloses
the after image
of his absent heart
where did he find
the toy sticks
he twirls in air
no longer
moved by the blind
angels lamenting the
ambiguity of their sex
Holbein created the dance
and went to his death

4

The angels invaded his space
their cries caused God
to freeze the sky
in order to stop
their harmonic fluctuations
Death threw his voice
upward in heat
creating heavenly fissures
where souls hid

5

God wore an apricot cloak
when he delivered Eve from Adam
a caesarean was performed
on Adam's torso
the moon is moved
by lips of severed heads
the sleep of Adam
is disturbed by
the screech of a peacock
a chameleon's blood
rushes to its head
absorbing all color
Death's too

6

While Eve waited
inside of Adam
she was his
structure
her volume
filled him
his skin hung
on Eve's form
when God
released her
from Adam
Death rushed in
preventing collapse

7

The feet of Adam
and of Eve bled
as they ran from
the pewter garden
Death followed
with his violin
God gave up his voice
to the heavens

8

Adam and Death
worked together
uprooted their first tree
dug their first grave
one sweated on his skin
the other on his bones
Adam imagined Death's structure
in his body

Death imagined Adam's skin
over him
where was the soul
to be placed?
Death wondered how
he was to put on Adam's skin
Adam could not feel the weight
of the skeleton
Eve uplifted her breast
to the flesh lips of the child
and hummed her first lullaby

9
Adam asked if
he could borrow
Death's hourglass
once in his hands
he turned it
upside down
Death was horrified

Eve smiled
and gave him a soul kiss

10
God hesitated
to ask Eve
if she loved
him

She refused to answer
since Adam was near

11
At dawn
Eve left the bed of Adam
in her nakedness
she crossed the grove
of olive trees
the dew on the iris stalks
moistened her thighs
the morning moon
reflected silver leaves
Death was waiting on the hill
red roses covered
his black robe and hood
she ran to him
and they embraced
Eve removed his habit
while he lifted her hair
he felt her breast
with his white hand
creating the meaning
of hard and soft
in silence she
loosened his grasp
and gently led him down
to the lake
where she wove honeysuckle
vines through his structure
the aroma became his skin
she placed her hand
within his chest cavity
and traced the contour
of an invisible heart
the palm bone
moved her convexity
she asked him to softly
lay his skull on her pelvis

she bent over him
and kissed the hollows
of his vanished eyes
and with her tongue
she forced him to open
he yielded her time
the seduction of Death
was complete

Adam awoke suddenly
his jealously evaporating

A splendidness prevailed

12
The objectivity of Death
had been compromised
he searched out
for the angels of annunciation
in order to explain
there was no movement of air
where they flew
he offered to give them
the hourglass as consolation
he knew that there was
no reasonable exit
he had fallen in love
with Eve

13
Death came upon
an open field covered
with sleeping angels
wings folded
over their faces
and locks of hair

Death was cold
and wanted one of them
he moved rapidly
towards their silence
quickly selected a youth
and with a single stroke
impaled him on his scythe
the others in panic
flew to God

14
He coaxes the matron
places his fingers
without flesh beneath
the armpit of the maiden
and feels her hair
through the linen
the carpenter swings
the ax at echoes
yet is taken anyway
sawdust blown into
vacant eye sockets
slivers of wood
wedged in leg joints
the Priest offers
an encyclical
for the passage
as he runs his tongue
over the enamel
of closed teeth
the removal of the skin
sheds Death

15
Eve wanted no less
than the soul of Death
she threw off
Adam's body
and offered herself
to God

16
Death made no sound
for fear of awakening God
he had emptied his hourglass
refilled it with
the souls of the suicides
a sleepless angel
discovered his act
flew down and encased him
in metallic wings
the shock
caused Death to let fall
his glass container
it shattered on earth
releasing its contents
which became the night

17
The dog snapped
at Death's ankles
Death pulled down
the bed covers
of his mistress
her gentle whispers
covered the ear
sockets which amplified
the wail within
he absorbed her negative

mock death as he plays
his bagpipe his breath
fills the cavity with
black humming birds
he is blind his eyes
had been removed
the inner underskin
molds our inverse
God asked for the suicide
of Death

18
Death's death was by
the inhalation of
all the souls
forgotten by the angels

Their tears flooded
his void

19
When Death's suicide
was announced to God
he closed the heavens
and nailed Death's coffin
with the stars of the night
and accompanied it to
the membrane of the sun
where the incineration of love
began instantaneously

20

Eve followed Death
soon after she heard
of his suicide
but first she returned
to the garden
and buried there
the whispers of all angels
which Death had entrusted
to her keeping
she removed the last leaves
made of pewter from the trees
and created
a pair of metal wings
she sewed them to her back
then began her flight
as she rose
discarding all earthly memories
on that day
the heavens rained blood

21

The shoots of spring
diminish the final cry
an angel of mercy
rides a wood wheel
sealing the soul
with a stitching

The opaque sound
is transmitted through
sand and clay
causing the crystallization
of the lament

The Breath of Bacchus

Your Carrara lips part
inhaling softly a whisper
which disappears
into the grey hollow
of a voided stone
your incised eyes
are bewildered
by the hush
within your mouth
the grapes of your hair
fall over your forehead
polished to a coldness
your creator made a miracle
through the surface
of his hands and wrists
he blew air into your
impenetrable white marble
producing the first
inanimate sigh
silencing all sound

Where Irises Once Were

Bruges' Madonna
the meeting of your lips
creates the crevice
of your Oriental smile
the lids of your eyes
are two slightly opened mouths
revealing hidden tongues
where irises once were
your faun nostrils contract
breathing inward
the future lament
erasing all signs
of the tears of blood

A Journey of Two

He and she
virgins two
knew no man
no woman
Nicodemus and
Magdalena
assisting the descent
his own mother's face
buried in his hair
as contortions exposed
muscle and bone
a dark quartet
in stone
aging simultaneously

You Once Were

You once were
inside of her
immaculate
now you lie
in her lap
made of thighs
both your heads
young
her massive right
hand supports
your imploded torso
a palm recently
punctured
holds the folded
marble cloth
of her robe
she balances
your death
it is hard
to believe
that she is
able to carry
your weight
now that it is
outside
your lips seem
to ask a
forgiveness

Your Breath Was Contained

Moments after your deposition
all sizes changed
you and Mary became old
her face thickened
toward a lament
your legs had atrophied
and your feet dragged
through the marble dust
all your weight had rushed
to your right arm
which had grown
twice its length
the agony had
swelled your lips
and at last
your breath was contained
inside
solidifying

Her Son's Face

Rondanini Pietà suspends
death's collapse
she holds up as she lowers
her son's face
hammered away into
a vagueness
he half smiles
at his mother's
touch
and at their
arisen descent
her eyes nose lips
flattened and rectangulated
determine the quality
of that gentle resurrection
and you?
you simply
evaporated into the heavens

Eros

Her chestnut-color hair
found painted in
Rembrandt's winter night
split down the center
falling vertically
on naked shoulders
covered in green velvet
his hands felt
the rejected electrons
as she gently swayed
her positioned body.

Her pale forehead required
Bronzino's thin silk ribbon
to mark the circumference
of her lover's thought
and to encircle
the hidden skull
his kiss dampened
the cloth's elasticity.

Her reflection witnessed
a deception
as she drew
into the mirror
the exaggeration of
an extended black eyebrow
the lids of her eyes
closed and opened
simultaneously
lubricating the lashes
towards a seduction
her cheeks revealed
a blush that made
desire wait.

Weightless Heart

She placed her nostrils
into the heart
of a flower
inhaling a vacancy
soft membrane of her lips
held their blood's transparency
her mouth opened
allowing for the commencement
of a ritual
her throat swallowed
all lingering echoes
as she adjusted
the earrings
her tongue moistened
the finger ends
he spoke her name
as he touched
the cylinder of her neck
she dropped the beaded necklace
between her breasts
their tips arched
in slow motion.

Her wrist and elbow
ran parallel to his
as her concave palm
closed over his convexity
the curvature
of her stomach
rivaled that of Ingres's Odalisque
male and female fingers
traced the contour
down
to separate the tangency
of her inner thighs.

He and she
coordinated their dreams
of northern Russia
as the white wolf
leaped past the bear
at that moment
the snakes of Pergamon
moved along the frieze
and Persephone wept
in the grey hall
her legs raised to
a dark fertility
her feet encased
by calfskins
dyed german blue
he searched for the seam
that would open her
and discovered
her negative
beginning the crossover.

She whispered to him
that her weightless heart
was floating within
her voided space
and that it needed structure
to become still
suddenly
he saw her
internal mold
brushed with warm fluids
clinging to her inverse
he offered himself to her
in order to see
through woman.

They exchanged themselves
and the earth
fell.

Soundings

He threw his voice
into the diminishing
perspective
as she receded
leaving him
an echo.

He drew her a rose
and nailed it to her coffin.

The shape of her eyes
were the shape of her mouth
forming a trilogy
he kissed her
her taste was of rust
she laughed
at his astonishment
his lips turned black.

She replied,
"Architect keep your
hard-edge geometry
I will keep my softness.

My breasts are
more beautiful
than church spires.

Feel my body
architect
so your plans
will not be so rigid

listen to the sound
of my voice
so you will know
what volume is
my soul is made
of no substance
your space might
be the same
I am made
for birth
and you?"

Whispers of Prague

City of whispers
you are dark
even when the sun shines
your river moves swiftly
over the deep crevices
of its buried topography
the drunken Japanese
shouts at the bridge angel
as the town cascades
down to the stone squares
where lovers open their lips.

The day train to Kutná Hora
is met by the man
with a double-breasted suit
leaning on a black Tatra
the girl waiting at the station
removes the milk bottle
from the dog's lips
and then licks its rim
Kafka was over six feet tall
and Rilke appeared preoccupied.

The trolley passes the clock tower
where the wedding couple smile and kiss
the iron gates of the Baroque church
are closed shut

your building stones entomb.

Munch's Night Crossing

He arranged the covers of the bed
and lay down naked on the white cloth
he imagined Marat taking a bath
she came through the oak door
into the plum-colored room
her black hair parted in the middle
remembering her not long ago puberty
she carried a brush glistening
with red paint she painted his wrists
as he stared at the flowers of the wallpaper
she moved her small breasts across his lips
which reminded him that he
must catch the night boat to Berlin
he asked her if she had seen the
photograph he had taken of himself.

The Panther of Potsdam

The panther escaped
from the Berlin Zoo
the director sent out
an order,
"The animal
was not to be harmed."
It was seen moving
along the lake edge.
The canal bargeman
offered his metal net
while people talked
the panther arrived
in Potsdam with
a pheasant in its mouth.

For the Berlin Painter

Her wound festered
as butterflies nibbled
at her shrunken soul
letters of the words
of the thought of revenge
dropped into her already
poisoned bloodstream
increasing the beat
of her thinning heart
her lips drained of moisture
extending the dryness
of woman's hate.

Anne

She almost had moved
completely into her darkness
when she faintly heard
his loving voice
pulling her back
through quiet implorations.
She with her last breath
pushed through the debris
of her memories
toward his heart of pain.

Lavina

Lavina hugged
the heavy porcelain plates
as she set the table
the smoke from the candelabra
passed over the portrait of Ezra
as he slid open the parlor doors
his eyes scanned the room
and rested on the silver cask
reflecting the roses on her breasts
she removed the knife from the drawer
and sliced the soft peach
as Orin uplifted his face
to suck the grapes.

The austerity of the house
hid the inner salaciousness.

Electra

Her mother's jealousy
flowed out of her
thick like the blood
of an ancient wound
balming his hatred
the mirror she held
reflected her opacities
solidifying the soul's
transparencies into ice
sending a coldness to
the chambers of her heart.

Seville Blue

Black veils thrown back
cascading down dark
Andalusian hair
her mantilla drapes across
firm Spanish breasts
the red waist sash
anticipating future
secret delights
she points to
brocaded shoes and to
the velvet
of the dress hem
challenging a lifting
her golden rings
to be removed
from fingers
that will gently touch
the skin
explaining night.

A Dead Oak

The nineteenth century
sucked out your eyes
as you sat on the limb
of a dead oak
with the elders
speaking through their
hands crouching
in night robes
they plucked you
forward towards
the winged horse
with Falcon head
you looked down
in the hope of a
retrieved vision
and knew your
two-headed sister
demanded your expulsion
while the others
danced their circle
chanting to the dusk's
flight as he
balanced on the wood pole
observing the river's flow
and the silence of the bull.

A Distant Breath

As she folds the fan
between her fingers
his eye pierces through
the magnifying glass
focusing on the swell
of her breast
while the other two
put on their silk shifts
to the soft laughter
of thoughts expectant
he cocks his hat
as she arches her back
her lace eye mask
the color of her pupils
the wind blows her
opaque shawl over
head and back
as she presses the skirt
down
between the contour
of her touching knees
the garters rolled
into ellipses
he stands fixed
by the sound
of a distant breath.

A Dark Plum Room

Her lover's thoughts about her
produced moisture on the mirror
clouding her reflection
she drew her face on
as he fingered the lock behind her ear
when she turned
he blew a kiss into her
then their bodies formed
a single contour line
inside curvatures
she remembered the
trio in a dark plum room.

Abduction

The old woman
watches her precise
movement
and thinks of past
seductions.
The young woman
holds up her long skirt
revealing
foot ankle calf knee
as she tightens
the stocking over
her taut skin.
Hastening
her kidnappers' desire
they touch her
simultaneously
raising her off the earth.
The hooded one
at her lower extremities
the other wraps his arms
around her torso
her black hair hangs
limp as her soft mouth
utters a desperation.
Her abductor's face
etched into
the night sky.

Under the Granite Arches

Suddenly . . .
she remembers
the iron balconies
and the feel of silk
. . . the aroma
of honeysuckle.

Their hands speak
another . . . language.

She implores their mercy
under the granite arches
of the aqueduct.

The others have already
been dragged from the light.

Devouring Angel

The angel flew down
within range
and like a porcupine
releasing its needles
shot all his feathers
into the hearts' blood
of the martyrs' torturers
to be spilled
staining the earth.

Obsession of Dürer

1

The etched soul
to him everlasting
the harmonic fluctuation
of his heart
for him a silent deposition
hear the slipping of his weight
her lament internal
landscape of sorrow
angel mother son

2

Creating Within Him

Adam wraps his arm
around the naked back of Eve
his hand slips below her breast
as she whispers into his ear
private sounds
his mouth parts for air
her convex stomach
rests above his upper thigh
the lion hides within
a black ink forest
boar and goat fixed still
Adam's and Eve's nipples touch
when the serpent
places in her uplifted hand
the explosive fruit
she brushes the golden sphere
horizontally along Adam's dry lips
creating within him memory

3

When the angel alights
on the sacred earth
its sword becomes heavy
anticipating the weight
of future sins
he pushes Adam and Eve
out
towards evermore guilt
as the garden recedes
the angel evaporates
and the first snow
falls
on the expelled rejected
beginning winter

4

The shepherds' knees bled
when they knelt in adoration
the wood shafts held
sprouted white chrysanthemums
the north star burst
showering the evergreens
with pellets of mercury
the wings of the angel
covered Joseph's cheek
and shielded the child
from the flames
of the sun

5

The angel spoke
a pregnant language
in order that her
fullness grew
she listened to
its completeness
and peered into
lavender eyes

6

He looks back
through the
particles of sand
and vaguely sees
her contour unfolding
he hears her voice
diminishing
in sounds like
the movement
of the palms
during a soft wind

7

He rides through
the granite arch
projecting a joined shadow
of man and animal
its edge dims
the light on the gold
a phosphorescence fills
the hall
and all laughter
dies down
a carpenter
builds the table
for the supper
a white cloth
is washed in the river

8
Former eclipses
foretold
agonies unimaginable
while he waited
in the garden

9
Judas places his kiss
the torches of the night
flicker
giving off black smoke
blinding the screeching
and covering the moon's light
the air is impregnated
with falling white blossoms
his thought withdraws

10
Annas
Caiaphas
Pilate
Herod
their souls
drowned in the
tears
of their mothers

Annas
Caiaphas
Pilate
Herod
your eyes sprouted
snakes

Annas
Caiaphas
Pilate
Herod
your lips sewn
together with
panther's gut

Your ears sealed

11
Five mockers
in perpetual
damnation
frozen within
their mocking
positions
waxen figures
with blood stained
inverted eyeballs
observing their own
internal maggots

12
They tied him
to a white marble
column
the stone was
so cold
that it stiffened
his skin
deflecting
the intensities
of the flagellators'
blows

13
The thorns
of the crown
dug into his head
as the vine stems
were pushed down
blood drops rose
upward when a
forked branch
was placed in his hands
three crosses of wood
were brought forward
as he was pushed to
the opening
and cuts were made
Pilate dipped and washed
his hands in a silver disc
and demanded more water
from the pewter jug
they pulled him
by the rope around his neck
to the cross

and ordered him to carry it

14
He fell
under the weight
of the inflicted
proddings
Veronica on her knees
held the cloth
before him
a transference
occurred
commencing a sacred
reference

15

The awl spiralled
the wood sliver up
as the peeling of the skin
of a fruit
iron pincers and spikes
lay on the earth
the horizontal member
of the wood cross
was supported at the ends
by two rocks
the nail was placed
at the center
of the palm
as the hammer was raised
the soldiers standing
indifferent

16

The simultaneity
of life leaving
and
of life giving
began at that
heart's blood draining

17

The ladder is positioned
upright against the cross
he slumps over
descending shoulders
held in place
by a pulley of fabric
the hand spikes
removed by a
double-clawed hammer
the foot nail is
gently slid out
and the women wait

18
Her hands open up
and part
as her lips
open emitting a sigh
recalling
the sound of
a receding wave

19
He was let down
into the tomb
the weight increased
at his descent
the hole in the cave
black beckoned

20
He wanders through air
saturated with waiting souls
insufficient pressure
to overcome their vacancies
they adhere to his
thoughts' remoteness
and faintly pump up
their past sins

21

His visitations
opened up
as his wound
to Thomas's hand
his ascension
completed his
journey on earth
and commenced
his heavenly
judgements

flower and sword

22
Death of the Virgin

When her soul
left her
content

A Lament

sight maximum extensions
from maximum compression
suction into a two-dimensional plane
the paradox of a planar flux
with a barrelling in
explosions and implosions
simultaneously
the peripheral cords
of a drum
at the edge
suspended skin
creating a resonance
when struck volumetric sound
of haunting opacities
the solidity of granite cylinders
florentine columnar greys
beyond the specific grey
the density of material
aura of opaque radiation
blocks as slabs of weight
occupying sliding shearing
slipping nudging magnifying
evaporating limited space
impenetrable
tap them
with a wooden mallet
and
hear the echoes of sound
trapped in stone
entombment of space
holds a syncopation
the cries of muffled brass
playing on time's frame
spiraling to a point
celebrating a sadness.

Chartres Dusk

The statues of Chartres
cursed the sculptors' craft
the masons had joined
their backs to
the stone cathedral
attaching the fate of subject
to object in
a limited eternity
the roof gargoyles
grinned from their perches
only the volumesound
of the organ
moved through their densities
the ascending hallelujah
moistened the aging surfaces
and washed away the ancient dust.

Rural Priest

He was a rural priest
they called
him Father
he said Mass
he heard
their confessions
he married
them
he baptized
their children
he buried
their dead
he walked through
their vine maze
he ate the food
they brought
him
he drank the wine from
their fields
he slept in the bed
they constructed for him
he opened the church doors
he talked to
them while
they sat on wooden pews
he contemplated the Stations of the Cross
they knelt and stood
they rang the bell
he looked up to the crucifixion
they looked up to the Virgin

he and
they descended to the crypt
he received the flowers
they gave
him
he watched the sun rise
he watched the sun set
he looked for the moon
he felt the rain
he smiled at the snow
he listened to the wind
he cherished the heat
he was refreshed by the cold
his voice gave comfort
when
he died
their voices sung the songs from
heaven
he had entered
their souls.

Hymn to a Sculptor

O Giacometti
maker of elongated thoughts
the thinnest of time
we praise your night phantoms
and the apparition wives
your signature of roughness.

An Evening Conversation

It's that the program
is not the usual one
What do you intend?
It could be called
a program of pessimism
A banker's program?
It's for the weekends
For weekends?
Particular ones
Would it include a fireplace?
Of course
One that could be sat around?
Not necessarily
The entry?
I want metal doors
10 x 10
approximately
I wish for reverberation
Reverberation?
That is the diminishing
of sound
A dining room?
Better a dining table
I envisioned it black
with edge reveals
In the living room?
It could be called
the other
A library?
One that one could
sing from
A bedroom?

If you wish to call
it that
A garage for the
Buggatti
and a shelf for
leather gloves
The garden?
I will provide
the stones
The kitchen?
Below
Have you considered
fluorescent lighting?
I prefer wall-hung
lamps six inches high
Ventilation?
I believe that would be
essential

For certain functions
a ramp is needed
Colors?
Muted soft
as if fog brushed it
Do you prefer views?
More looking in
A roof garden?
Definitely
but no hand rails
I wish to install roses
What will you do with
the paintings?
Store them
When would you wish to begin?
We have already.

Investigation of a Museum

The granite pharaohs
plotting their own escape
from the museum
the pewter ibis
gliding through the Egyptian hall
fluorescent marble panther
leaping
on the glass faun
shattering it to shards.
The ivory snake
blood-stained
by the slivers
The painting on Nefertite's face
blistering
as hyenas suck
her wax tits
The flesh of man
a sacrilege
in such a place.

Archaeological Museum

Greeks

Why did you not reveal
that your gorgons
that your sirens
that your harpies
and your winged creatures
were unimaginable
they lived as you

Medusa smiled since
Athena knew why
Poseidon lost his eyes

The rooms are cold
and the guards
plug in the electric heaters
to take the chill
off their reality.

Acropolis

Your departures
and
your erasures
left
your vagueness

Snails live in
the crevices of
your shattered marble

Your heart pumps thoughts
incomparable

Exit implies entry's lament.

Medusa

No mythologies can elaborate
the pain at the roots
your horror comes
when the serpents sleep
it is then
that they become glazed
in salt
it is then too
that your mouth and eyes
open
simultaneously.

Sentences on the House and Other Sentences

I

A woman lives in the house; she has taken its name.

A house knows who loves it.

An empty house is one that metamorphoses into vacant space.

The breath of a house is the sound of voices within.

I sense I am leaving you.

I loved you in/a/way.

Forever is everfor.

Maze Gods the soul.

Maze guards the body.

The house is a nocturnal thing; this is seen from the out side
    when the lights are turned on.

The house is like a black cat at night, only a silhouette.

A house roams at night when its occupants sleep.

Night dreams are accelerated in fixed rooms.

Day dreams blank out light.

The yawning of a house comes from the excessive sound of
    its inhabitants.

The house likes the weaver; it remembers its early construction.

The sister of a house is its garden.

When a house is sad its glazing clouds over and there is no
    movement of air.

The house never forgets the sound of its original occupants.

A house's ghosts stay inside; if they leave and go outside they
    disappear.

A house is only afraid of gods, fire, wind, and silence.

A house's blood is the moving people within when they still stop.

A house is seen crying when it sheds its rainwaters.

The gods are jealous of the house because the house cannot fly.

The stairs of a house are mysterious because they move up and
    down at the same time.

Snow is female, icicles male.

A house fears the wind and is afraid of trees.

A house carries its own weight, also the sorrows within.

Lightning is the house's direct connection to the heavens.

God gave man two houses, his body and his soul.

All souls implode when a woman dies; it is then when man's heart disappears.

The sanctuary of a house is the closed room.

Man gave names to rooms, God gave the space.

The sound of a house is its distant lament.

The furniture of a house is the silent witness of man.

The house doorknob inverts time.

The aroma of a room is defined by woman's presence and by her absence.

A house's shadow proves its dark two-dimensionality.

A house's calendar is its internal falling leaves.

Crawling vines on a house hint at its agelessness.

When a woman's dress falls on the floor of a room God hears it.

The birth of a house is from a female.

To dance in a house is forbidden fruit.

A house awaits letters.

A house's windows yearn for the sun.

Frosted windows are the drawing boards of a house.

A porch of a house mediates between nature and building.

A house lies in state during wars.

Flowered wallpaper within a house makes the house feel an unease.

Locked doors within a house mean either joy or horror.

The stone floors of a house in winter send a chill to all extremities.

The thoughts of a private house should be kept secret.

Heat rises in a house in order to return to mother sun.

God named house.

The soul of a house is its soul.

The awnings of a house indicate a house's sorrow.

Moonlight within a house is the darkest light imaginable.

A house wakes up in the morning and smiles at the bird feeder.

Night stars are an indication that it is snowing in the universe.

A red dawn makes the house drowsy.

A house plays with the lake through its reflections.

The wind blows the leaves off a tree because it wants to see
     it naked.
Moonlight reveals to the house that other houses have souls.
A house closes its eyes when it is being renovated.
A house knows that there is inevitable surgery in store for it.
Tree roots are relatives of a house's foundation.
Illuminated clouds are God's quiet thoughts reflected.
A woman unfolds as a house of many rooms.
A woman moves through the house as angels move through
     the air.
When a woman combs her hair a house becomes entirely silent.
The carpets of a house are the slippers of a house.
A woman washes her body as moonlight washes a house softly.
A woman's voice is as varied as a long day's light in a room.
When a woman washes the glass of a window she washes away
     God's discarded thoughts.
A woman's lips close as the curtains of a house close to be
     opened in the dawn.
A cat in the house is the silent surveyor.
The books in the library of a house age with the inhabitants
     of the house.
When two lovers speak in a room the air listens.
The bookshelves of a house store past and present loves and
     wait for future volumes.
A bowl of fruit on a table in a room adds a touch of volumetric
     pigment.
She wrapped her arms around the wood column and imagined
     the earlier tree.
A thatched roof is the house's shawl.
A woman's eyes looking through an open slat of a shutter make
     the peacock's eyes plausible.
The hands of the old painter gripped the wood handrail in
     order to support his solid vision.
The studio of a painter is for painting and other things, too.
The painter embalms death.
When a woman rocks a child in her arms Death becomes
     bewildered.

When a woman blows a kiss in a house it lingers.

The eyes of the players of a string quartet in a room meet and exchange themselves and their hearts.

A house is born, lives, and dies and is named house.

The house gains immortality when it becomes only a thought that ceases to exist.

God punishes the house by withdrawing its time.

Snakes enter a house in order to escape God's wrath.

Wild geese fly in a triangle to puncture the clouds.

The heaviness of the granite of a house comes from the stone's absorption of the house's melancholy.

Moisture on the stones of a house forms from the house's fear of fog.

Curtains of a house are its veils; when removed, a glimpse of a house's nakedness is revealed.

A house is a woman's sexual collaborator, filled with private thoughts.

Air is invited in when a woman opens a window.

Books are female; a mysterious ritual lies within them.

The sound of books can only be heard internally.

An abandoned house is God's warning and death's forsakenness.

A woman moving down a stair in a house is slow-detemined.

The earrings of a house are the suspended flowerpots on a porch.

The spider webs on a house are the cataracts of the house.

The tablecloth is thrilled by the touch of plates and awaits further violations.

The china closet senses all the lips that have touched its inhabitants.

The house acts as the recovery room for broken cups and soiled antiques.

The cellar is the bowels of a house; it collects all wastes and discarded time.

The bed in a house promises future joys and remembers past sorrows.

A forlorn house is a house without a woman.

A woman moves her fingers over the surface of a pewter jug and thinks of man.

A house is suspicious when an armoire is introduced to an unfulfilled room.

A sudden draft in a room is from the sigh of the house.

A house wants to be alone with a woman intimately.

A house contemplates the internal thickness of the fruit in a bowl.

Candlelight is the house's passing thought.

Hail falling on the glass windows of a house is the suicide's afterthoughts.

Angels carry soulfilaments on their wings.

The house searches for its lost occupants.

The house objects to the sea's fluidity.

The sea coaxes the house into its undertow.

God created house to contain man's sins.

A wall anticipates nails being driven into it; paintings cover the punctures.

The knife and fork distanced man's tactility.

A floor carries all the house's vanished footprints.

The sudden appearance of a woman in a door frame takes the breath away.

The bowl receives the soup as a celebration to all concavities.

Milk flowing from a pewter pitcher hints at a woman's thought—fluid, metallic, opaque, rich, silent movement.

When a woman wraps a long scarf around her neck the nineteenth century comes into view.

A woman reading a book is different from a man reading a book.

Dusk is woman's possession of the house.

A house blushes when a woman pins up her hair.

Wallpaper is the house's internal dress.

The house receives hidden letters, photographs, and secret thoughts.

Drawers containing silk garments are the coffins of past sins.

Clothes hanging in a closet are collapsed volumes.

A woman writing at a desk is the house's three-dimensional painting.

The rulers of a house are its mirrors; time is measured and judged.
A polished marble table feels like the skin of a plum and of
     other skins, too.
A ceiling fan keeps angels from entering a room.
A house feels pleasure when a woman ties a ribbon in her hair.
Curtains blowing in a room are caused by the kiss of the wind.
Moldings hide the wounds of a house.
The leaves of the mimosa tree close their eyes at night.
A woman bites at the sewing thread as a cat bites at the neck of a
     bird—ferocious joy.
A woman hums day's soul away and welcomes night's silences.
The painter is God's photographer.
The buds of spring push up through the earth as fingers of dead
     life.
God flattens three dimensions into the surface of a canvas
     to still life.

II

Death waits living on our time.
Our death is outside of us.
The death of a house is announced by the only standing structure
     —the brick chimney.
The attic of a house is where children go and where Death hides.
The roof shingles of a house absorb God's heat during the
     day and Death's chill during the night.
The height of a door of a house is for man's entry; the width of a
     door of a house is for man's exit: one dimension for life, the
     other dimension for death.
Death demands that houses have windows so that he can see day
     and night simultaneously.
Death is pleased when man cuts flowers; he sees the act as a
     premonition.
Death is nothing compared to life.
Death hates film negatives.
We never see the last card of death until it is over.

Death inculcates us with dread, then erases the r.

Death argues with God about the vertical while man lies
horizontal.

Death's favorite color is the rose.

The poet's words are incomprehensible to Death.

The house welcomes Death after it has lived its life.

Death asked God for his house.

Death glides on the hinges of house doors.

Death covers his bones with wet plaster in order to lubricate his
dryness.

The closets of the house enclose the cloth of death.

Death is monochromatic, like Hawthorne's soul.

The noise of death is the whispers in other rooms.

Death knocks on the entry door of a house when the sound
is not to be heard.

Death is always jealous of woman.

Death rests under the footings of the house.

The mirrors of a house are covered by Death.

Death is disliked because he takes away breath.

White walls of a house make death vague when Death is naked.

Death's laugh becomes man's cry.

The threshold of a house makes Death pause.

A house is preparation for death in that it encloses.

The floors of a house are washed and polished in order to make
Death's blood soft.

Skylights are built for winter flowers, which Death cultivates.

Flowers in a room have two purposes, to sweeten life and death.

The windowsill prevents man's fall and assists Death's entry.

A drapery is the shroud of a window.

The window shade is Death's sign.

When dogs bark at a corner in a room they provoke Death's
triangle.

Mirrors become opaque at the moment of death.

To live with death is possible, to live in death impossible.

With a death a house changes forever.

A wreath on a house door announces Christmas and death.

Death perches on the peak of a house's roof.

The shutters of a house of a suicide are always closed.

Cold air slips under the door of a house as a sense of future deaths.

Singing within a house arouses angels and makes Death wait for a moment.

Death implores the house to open its doors.

The house can hear death by its total silence.

The sun is a friend of death in that it bleaches the color out of a house's paintings.

When a woman smiles in a house, Death tries to imitate her.

Death's painting in a house is a still life.

A sudden death shows Death's impatience.

A rocking chair in a house induces Death to be quiet.

The sighing of a house makes Death change direction.

The first nail driven into a wood post of a house makes Death rejoice.

A house waits for daylight as Death waits for darkness.

Moonlight and Death are the sisters of the afterglow.

The bird of death flies through the wallpaper of a plum colored room.

When Death sleeps the earth dances.

God banished Death from his house in order to see the light.

Death's skull is the house of black birds; they enter the house through the eye sockets.

Death brought the color of black to earth's houses.

Death needed black cloth to cover the whiteness of his bone.

White is the undercoat of Death's house.

Death builds his city underneath.

Death scrubs the body until it looks like him.

God takes everything above the earth; Death takes every thing below the earth.

A flower vase becomes life; a funeral urn becomes death.

When it snows, Death requests his black cloak; he believes in the extreme condition.

God threatens the fires of hell when he becomes sad with the earth.

When a man builds a house God overwatches; when a man
    destroys a house Death undersees.
Death is only structure.
Death wants the skin of the house.
Death's lifelong workshop is man's body; God's is man's soul.
A woman stares at Death's skull until the eye sockets of Death
    are filled with blood.
A woman holds Death's skull to her breasts until Death softens.
A woman invites Death into the house, then proceeds to
    break his bones.
A woman puts Death's cloak on in order to whiten her skin
    and darken her eyes.
A woman forces Death's teeth open with the stem of a rose.
Death makes a wreath of roses and rose stems blood red.
Death watches the wild geese trapped within the arabesque
    of the wallpaper.
Death's dimension is one.